#BabyLove

My Toddler Life

Written & Illustrated by
Corine Dehghanpisheh

FOR PARENTS WHO
CHERISH SPECIAL MOMENTS.

#BabyLove: My Toddler Life

Published by My Art to Inspire
P.O. Box 30302 NY, NY 10011

Designed By: Paula Riley

ISBN: 978-0-9978985-0-7

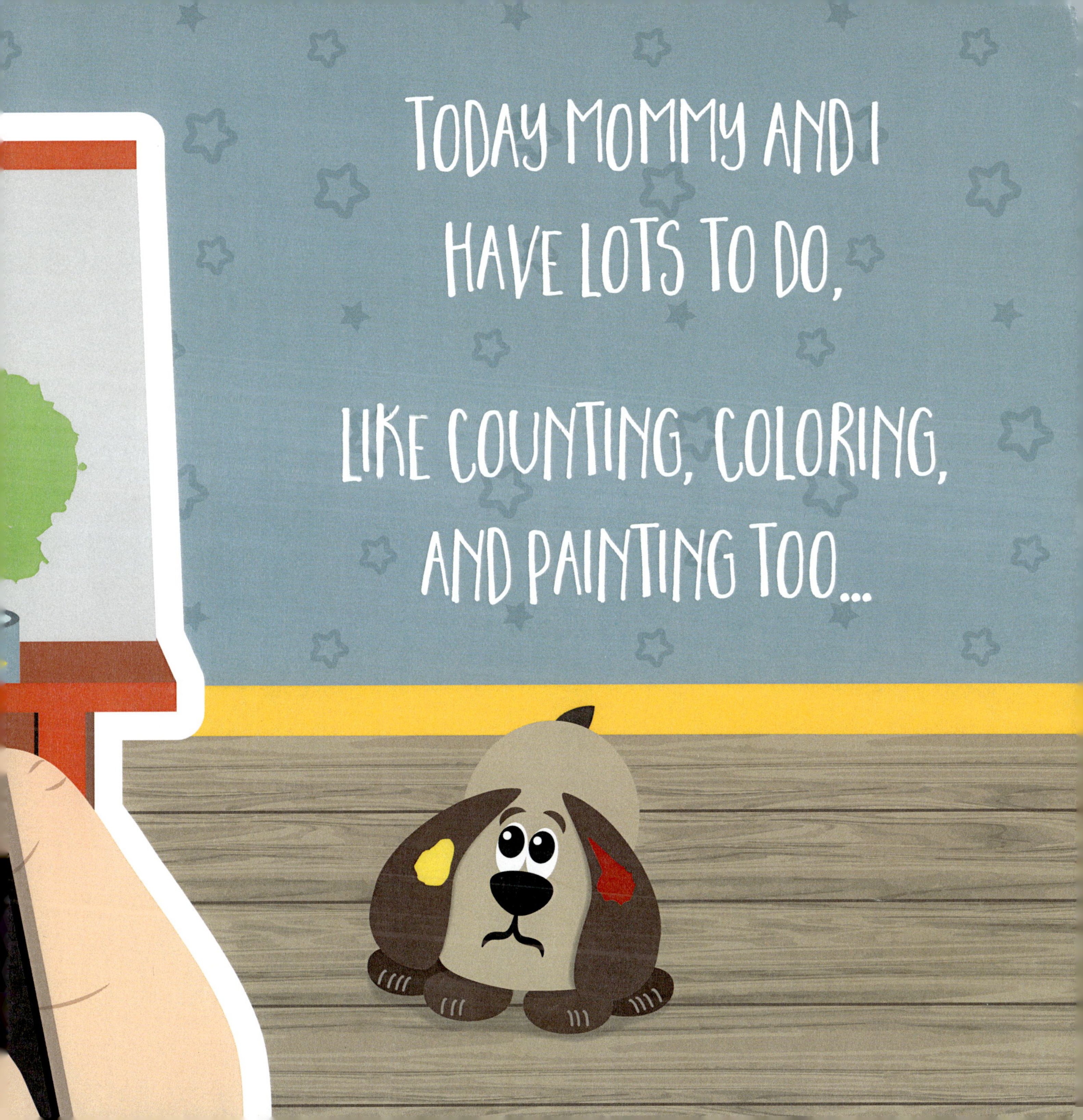

Today Mommy and I
have lots to do,

like counting, coloring,
and painting too...

BLOCKS
TRUCKS
TOYS
BEARS
Farms
BAA
Panoramic
Photo
Video

READING BOOKS,
PLAYING WITH TOYS,

LEARNING NEW WORDS, AND MAKING

NOISE!

OFF 00:00:19
Panoramic

Love my family. #mommyandme #toddlerlife
36
4

WE RECORD OUR FUN
FOR FRIENDS TO SEE.

POSTING THE PICTURES:
#MOMMYANDME.

WHEN NO ONE IS LOOKING,
I FIND MOMMY'S PHONE.

IT'S NOT MINE; I SHOULD
LEAVE IT ALONE.

BUT...

I PICK IT UP AND
HOLD IT TO MY EAR.

"HELLO! HELLO!"
I SHOUT,
THEN DISAPPEAR.

I CLIMB AND HIDE IN MY BIG RED CHAIR,

TAKING MY SELFIE FOR MOMMY TO SHARE.

I HOLD A BUTTON,

AND THEN SAY "CHEESE."

I CLICK, CLICK, CLICK, CLICK

WITH SUCH EASE.

SHUFFLE, SHUFFLE.

UH-OH!

I HEAR A SOUND!
I RUN, DROPPING THE PHONE
TO THE GROUND.

"NO, NO." I HEAR MOMMY SAY.

"THAT'S MY PHONE.
IT'S NOT FOR PLAY."

"SORRY, MOMMY," I SAY WITH A FROWN.

Video
Photo
Panoramic

"THANK YOU," SHE SAYS.
"NOW, PLEASE SIT DOWN."

"LET'S LOOK AT YOUR PICTURES. WHAT DO YOU SEE?"

"MY EYES, MY HAIR,
MY MOUTH, MY FACE..."

Video
Photo
Panoramic

"I See Me!"

"YES, THAT IS YOU!

BIG AND STRONG, AND VERY WISE.

PLAYFUL, LOVING,
AND FULL OF SURPRISE."

CARS
TRUC
BEARS
QUACK!
Video
Photo

6
months old
Photo
Panoramic

"YOU HAVE GROWN SO FAST.
HOW CAN THAT BE?

TIME GOES BY TOO QUICKLY—
ONE DAY, YOU'LL SEE."

utdoor fun. #MommyDate
206
24
Photo
Panoramic
#AquariumFun
52
6

"I LOVE YOU SO MUCH,
TOO MUCH TO MEASURE.

THESE MOMENTS WITH YOU,
I LOVE AND TREASURE."

A HUG FOR MOMMY,
THEN WE ARE ON OUR WAY.

WE PUT DOWN THE PHONE
AND START TO PLAY.

48923943R00024

Made in the USA
San Bernardino, CA
08 May 2017